Manifest Soulmate Love:
8 Essential Steps to Attract Your Beloved

Embark On A Journey of Inner Transformation to Prepare

for Your Ultimate Spiritual Partner

By International Spiritual Coach & Healer

Syma Kharal

To my beloved soulmate, Eric.

Table of Contents

Introduction

"All the particles of the world are in love and looking for lovers."

~ Rumi

Beautiful Beloved, before I share anything, I must congratulate you on your decision to manifest *soulmate love*. The desire to find our beloved is a spiritual call, because it is the eternal inner call that propels us to return "home" to our true state of perfect divine love and bliss. The call is one soul's sacred intention to experience and express its own essential nature of pure, unconditional love with another matching soul that is ready for the same.

However, I know from personal and professional experience that until we recognize, heal, and transcend our greatest inner barriers to such profound love, we will continue to experience painful patterns that keep us stuck in confusion, frustration, longing, and loneliness. My own journey to soulmate love is a testament to this.

My Journey to Soulmate Love

In spite of a tumultuous childhood and teen years filled with every form of abuse, I always believed in the magic and power of true love. But I also knew that I had to first become my own heroine, as I faced many battles throughout adolescence.

The physical and emotional abuse I incurred from my parents, paired with the sexual abuse I experienced from "family friends," led me to begin my healing journey at the age of fourteen. I was severely depressed and experiencing painful symptoms of post-traumatic stress disorder, and with no family support available, I turned to Spirit for help.

In the midst of my immersion into spiritual therapies and books, one day I came across Rumi's beautiful poem:

"From the moment I heard my first love story, I started looking for you, not knowing how blind that was. Lovers don't finally meet one day, they are in each other all along."

Even though I was fourteen at the time, I felt like the Divine had whispered that poem right into my heart, assuring me that as I find my way back to wholeness and light, there would be a great love waiting for me on my path.

I spent the rest of my teens and early twenties becoming a peaceful warrior and fighting many religious, cultural, and parental barriers to take a stand for myself and my siblings. I was able to end the cycle of abuse, refused to be forced into an arranged marriage, fought to pursue post-secondary education, and paved the way for my three younger sisters to do the same.

In addition to these triumphs, I successfully graduated with an Honors Degree in Psychology with distinction from one of Canada's top universities and two years later, I earned a post graduate certificate in corporate communications with high distinction.

After launching my career at one of the world's best PR firms, I decided I was finally ready to meet "the one." Instead— from seemingly nowhere—I was hit with a second major bout of depression.

This came as a huge shock to me, because I had already done so much transformational work to get to where I was. But I very quickly realized that while I had overcome a lot of challenges, there were much deeper unconscious and even karmic patterns that I still needed to confront and heal.

Ideally, I would have had a loving partner by my side to support me through this second dark night of the soul. Instead, what I manifested was a very disempowering relationship with a long-time friend who was in an even darker place.

He had bipolar disorder, an alcohol problem, a mistrust of women, and a deep fear of intimacy and commitment. In spite of his mental illness, he had been a warm, sweet, and thoughtful friend. But as soon as we entered a relationship—which he himself initiated—his fears surfaced full-force, and he became cold, distant, and disrespectful.

I ended up feeling far worse with him than I already had on my own. Eventually, he confessed that he had just wanted to "explore" being more than friends, but realized that the relationship—or as far as I saw it, *I*—wasn't for him. I was completely devastated. His rejection left me feeling utterly unworthy and abandoned. I hit complete rock bottom and felt entirely alone . . . until I realized I wasn't alone at all.

In the depths of my despair, I heard the clearest call from Spirit that *It* was the rock I fell on. *It* was holding me. Realizing this, I knew that I would find all the strength, guidance, and tools I needed to build a new foundation for myself, one formed from my own divine truth and power. I made a pact with the Divine that I would spend the next three months doing everything I could to completely transform my life.

That very night, I attended a Kundalini yoga class where the teacher shared specific *mantras* (sacred sounds), *mudras* (sacred hand gestures), *pranayama* (breathing techniques) and *asanas* (yoga postures) that help treat depression. I knew this was the Divine's blessed initiation. It was the beginning of the rebuilding.

I spent the next ninety days absorbed in intensive spiritual healing and practices, no matter how new age some of them first seemed: past life-regressions, working with angels and goddesses, cord-cutting, sage smudging, karmic healing, Akashic records healing, inner child healing, chakra healing, crystal healing, daily meditations, affirmations, mantras, yoga, Reiki, aromatherapy, feng shui—you name it, I did it.

In the process, I realized that I wasn't just healing from the deeper effects of the trauma and abuse of my past: I was uncovering and clearing karmic patterns that stemmed back many lifetimes. Layers upon layers of pain and untruth were shedding away. And the deep, heavy darkness that had consumed me slowly started to lighten.

By the end of the three months, I was no longer surviving: I was thriving. I was glowing. I was frolicking. I had healed my inner girl and unleashed my inner goddess. I was centered in my inherent joy, power, and truth. I had reconnected with my infinite, eternal, sacred self-worth and value. I was in love with myself and with life—with every little thing and with the entire universe.

That's when the magic happened. I was busy buying myself flowers, taking weekend trips with friends, and learning everything I always wanted to (painting, fencing, swimming, belly dancing, etc.). I was also training and being certified in spiritual healing methods, spending time in service to others, and relishing every moment like it was a sacred gift. And then I saw Eric.

I had actually seen him around before, as he was a friend of a friend's, but I never really *saw* him until I was ready. In fact, I later found out that Eric had a crush on me for the entire year I was dating my old friend and then working on myself. But in spite of his charming and respectful attempts to pursue me, I was just unable to connect with him.

I realized only later that, while he had already done so much spiritual work on his own journey and was ready for soulmate love, I had not been ready for it or for him. He was so connected to his joy, his power, his wisdom and true self, that my heavy

4

energy was not yet in alignment with his light. It wasn't until I had elevated my inner and outer states to where his already were that I finally saw him, noticed him, felt him, and opened to him. And as soon as I did, the magic unfolded and has been flowing ever since.

We watched the sun melt into the sky over the lake on our first date, and shared our first kiss under a full, golden-pink, autumn blush moon. We were connected in mind, body, heart, and spirit in that sacred moment; and it truly and completely felt like we were in heaven. Eric proposed at the same spot two years later, and we were married exactly a year after—on the third anniversary of our first date. We kissed for the first time as husband and wife on the same rocks where we shared our first kiss.

Since our lives were blessedly joined, we have loved, cherished, and adored each other every single day. We have supported and empowered each other to do and achieve things we may never have dared to dream on our own. This includes leaving toxic corporate careers to fully commit to our true callings and moving from frosty, fast-paced Toronto to enchanting Chiang Mai in tropical Thailand.

Our life here is beyond anything we could have envisioned. Eric greets me every morning with a garland of jasmine flowers and marigolds for my altars. He has warm lemon water, a fresh cut coconut and breakfast prepared for me to start the day. We spend our days doing the work we love, supporting each other through the challenges, and celebrating every little success as if it were a huge milestone.

We have our own spiritual practices and regularly take on forty-day ones as a couple. We give each other time and space to pursue our own passions, and love to share anything and everything as well—from tantra classes to traveling the world. We always communicate with love, affection, and respect. We feel safe in sharing our deepest insecurities and fears, and hold each others' vulnerabilities with compassion and tenderness. We still can't keep our hands off of each other, much to the chagrin of those around us. We are both equally committed to expanding our personal horizons and living out our highest purposes, both as individuals and as a couple.

Of course, we have had growing pains along the way and experienced challenges. But because of the spiritual work we did before and continue doing each day, our commitment to our personal growth and each others' highest good always prevails over the dramas and fears of our egos.

Eric makes me feel like a goddess every day. But it was *I* who first had to become the goddess he adores. I had to recover my spiritual self and reclaim my sacred feminine strength as a fully realized woman—not just the self-love and sensuality of Aphrodite, but the power of Kali, the wisdom of Sophia, the compassion of Kuan Yin, the strength of Sekhmet, the confidence of Hera, the intuition of Isis, the independence of Athena, and the focus of Artemis—and so many more.

It was only once I healed my deepest wounds and became not just the heroine of my own story, but unleashed the endless goddess gifts within, that I was blessed to manifest a man as equally his own hero and centered in his own divine masculine power.

I know with all my heart and soul that we were, as Rumi so eloquently said, "in each other all along," and that the love we are blessed with is the heavenly reward for the hell we went through before we could unite. Still, it was through our own personal journeys—all the growth and lessons we gained independently—that led to the triumph of the love and life we have come to share and build together. We both learned to become our own beloveds before becoming each others'. And I wouldn't have it any other way.

So, Beloved, no matter where you may be on your journey to love—no matter how many heartbreaks, tears, or dark nights of the soul you may have faced—I can assure you that if you are willing to do the inner work, face your darkest fears, heal your deepest wounds, release your most painful patterns, cultivate true self-love and partner with the Divine to manifest your soulmate, you will place yourself in perfect alignment for mastering the sacred keys to inviting divine love—which, once found, forever uplifts and blesses our journeys as we continue to heal, grow, and flourish together.

How to Use This Book

The steps you are about to learn will guide you on an empowering and transformational path to heal the inner barriers and create the right spiritual, emotional, mental, energetic and practical conditions to fully align with and invite soulmate love into your life. Each progressive section captures the essence of the eight intensive modules from my private "90-Day Manifest Soulmate Love Transformation Program" that I offer to only a select number of highly committed clients.

This program is already an intensely researched, divinely inspired, and strategically structured culmination of the most powerful practices for inner healing and outer manifesting. As such, I have witnessed it bring miracles not only in soulmate love, but in self-love, abundance, dream opportunities, and spiritual growth to my clients.

Due to the beautiful blessings the program has brought, I have deeply desired and been inspired to share its key teachings to many more in a way that is accessible and impactful. While the program modules expand extensively on each of the steps ahead and include my personal coaching and channeled guided meditations, my intention with this book is for you to feel equally supported as we embark on this journey together.

I wrote it while imagining myself present with you, lovingly taking you through an inner spiritual journey of self-discovery, healing, and transformation, so that you may come to know and love your own soul while you prepare to manifest your ultimate soulmate. As I share the principles and teachings of each advancing step, I will also include coaching questions or powerful practices to facilitate your progress.

At the end of our journey, I share Manifest Soulmate Love Affirmations to give you one more tangible and empowering tool on your path. I recommend starting them only after you complete all the steps, as affirmations are best used when your subconscious is receptive to their messages. In that chapter, I will also share instructions on how you can download a complimentary MP3 recording of the affirmations I created for you as a gift.

For now, here are some guidelines that will help you get the most out of your journey ahead and experience the highest possibility it holds for you:

- Follow each step progressively, even if you feel you are ready to start somewhere else.
- Give yourself space and time after each step to complete the suggested practices.
- Keep a journal and pen handy to answer the coaching questions and write your own reflections.
- Even if you want to skip forward, it is best to first do any recommended exercises.
- Since this is, above all, a spiritual journey, terms like "Spirit," "Universe," "God," and "the Divine" will be used interchangeably to represent the greater spirit, but please interpret them in the way that you best relate to, as no particular spiritual or religious association is intended.
- Take your time with each step. You may breeze through some, but others will call for you to slow down, reflect, and commit to deep healing. Please be very gentle and patient with yourself and the process.

- Enjoy the journey! Celebrate each step you complete because healing your blocks, reconnecting with your spirit, and preparing for soulmate love is no small feat.

I am so grateful that you have entrusted me with being your guide on this journey. I hope that you will feel my love and support in every word and with each step. I am holding the highest vision for you in preparing for the divine, blissful, soulmate love you desire and have always deserved.

I know that the entire universe is ready to bring it to you as soon as you are ready to receive it, and that is what we are going to do!

May your path to love be blessed in all ways.

All my love,
Syma

Step 1:

Establish Your Soulmate Love-Readiness

"Do the difficult things while they are easy and do the great things while they are small. A journey of a thousand miles must begin with a single step."

~ Lao Tzu

Okay, Beloved. We already know that you are looking for soulmate love, but are you actually ready for it? The answer might surprise you. When I take my program clients through their first guided meditation to experience the soulmate love meant for them, they are often completely shocked to discover how scared, resistant, and overwhelmed they feel when they get just a glimpse of the ultimate soulmate love waiting for them. This illuminates a very common cause behind our struggles in manifesting love:

Just because we are looking for love, doesn't mean we are ready for it.

To understand if and how this applies to you, the first step in preparing for love is to discover your *soulmate love readiness*.

This includes some key areas to consider to gain a clear perspective, such as your current emotional, mental, and spiritual state; your relationship with yourself; the relationship patterns and struggles you have experienced so far and how these struggles are impacting you; why you want a soulmate relationship; what you feel needs to happen to manifest your soulmate; and how your life would be different once you are together.

Before you start the inner work, you need to know what exactly to work on. On one hand, you could be desiring soulmate love with all your heart but harbor even stronger conflicting and sabotaging intentions within. On the other hand, you could be completely emotionally and spiritually ready and just need some guidance through the manifestation process.

In either case, it is essential to know where you are right now on your path in order to get a clear picture of your starting point. Often when we are searching for love or trying to manifest anything, we can get so caught up in our struggles—in what's not working and what's missing—that we get stuck, frustrated, and doubtful; instead of clear, open and optimistic. And we definitely need to be in the latter state in order to manifest our desires.

Although it can be challenging to do an honest assessment of where we have been, where we are, and where we want to be, this is an essential preliminary step before we can move forward in manifesting soulmate love.

This is why I ask the following questions before working with my clients on the program, and why I invite you to take some time to delve into them and determine where you are on your own quest for love:

Coaching Questions

1. What does soulmate love mean to you?
2. Where are you right now on your journey to manifesting soulmate love?
3. What is the main struggle you have been experiencing in manifesting soulmate love?
4. How is this impacting you internally: emotionally, mentally, spiritually, with your happiness, confidence, and overall fulfillment?
5. How is this impacting you externally: in your health and well-being, lifestyle, dreams and goals, other relationships, work, hobbies etc.?
6. What do you feel needs to happen for you to manifest soulmate love?
7. What is your relationship like with yourself?
8. How will your life be different once you are with your soulmate?
9. Why is this important to you?
10. What have you already tried to manifest soulmate love?
11. Do you feel prepared and ready to fully welcome soulmate love if it showed up today?
12. Are you ready and willing to commit to the inner work required to heal and transform self-sabotaging patterns and manifest the love you deserve?

I hope you answered yes to that last one! These questions will serve as a great start to help you clearly establish where you are right now, and where you need to be to prepare for and embrace the divine love you deserve. Once you know where you are, we can help you get to where you want to go: true soulmate love and happiness in all ways.

Step 2:

Understand What Soulmate Love Is (And What It Isn't)

"Some people come into your life as blessings. Others come into your life as lessons."

~ Mother Teresa

How did you answer the question, "What does soulmate love mean to you?"

Often when we think of soulmate love, we envision being with a partner with whom we share an incredible, euphoric connection, who fits and fulfills us in all ways, one who may possess a long list of qualities and characteristics we desire, and ultimately, someone who makes us feel loved, complete, and blissful.

However, one of the first things to understand is:

Your soulmate is not someone who completes you, but someone who complements you.

Understanding this distinction is essential in aligning your energy with the most evolved partner. The reason for this is that we don't just have one soulmate—we have many, and they are ready and waiting to show up in our lives to contribute to our mutual spiritual growth.

The soulmate love we all seek is the love of the highest, most evolved and harmonious partnership we can manifest. We want a love and a partner where we feel at home: blissful and connected on all levels, as we live our lives supporting, honoring, loving each other and continuously growing.

However, because we have many potential partners, the soulmate we attract will be the one best suited for the *soul-lessons* that we need to learn at that point of our lives. To distinguish between the two, we can refer to the first as our *ultimate soulmate* and the others as our *soul-lesson mates*. (Even though, from a spiritual perspective, everyone is a soulmate!)

While we may seek unconditional love from a soulmate, if we have not yet learned to love ourselves without condition, if we feel unworthy of such love and/or have not yet done the inner work required to receive such love, we may first attract a soul-lesson mate who is elusive and withdrawn. This is our own soul's benevolent but "tough love" way of pushing us to learn to love ourselves more than our need to earn the approval and acceptance of someone else.

To try and manifest a soulmate in hopes that they will relieve us of our loneliness or despair projects a heavy and needy energy that will push away the soulful partner we desire, and instead, attract partners who will push our lessons onto us.

In the case with my relationship with my old friend, for example, I was desperately seeking relief from feeling utterly empty and broken. However, instead of focusing on my own healing, I contributed to a dysfunctional dynamic that was not present when we were friends. I started playing the role of pleaser and rescuer, while he became the addict and victim.

I misguidedly took it upon myself to become "the one" who would help him believe in love, open his heart, and want to commit. I only later realized how unconsciously selfish this was on my part, because all my apparently "selfless" efforts stemmed from my own need to feel special, worthy, whole, and valued.

Thankfully, the eventual breakup led me to the path I needed to follow to learn the invaluable lessons of true self-love, -worth, and -value. And it was only after reconnecting with and claiming these that I came into vibrational alignment with my ultimate soulmate, my husband Eric, who had been ready for me for months.

If we don't learn the lessons we are meant to learn, then even if we end the relationship, we may continue to experience the same pattern in our next ones, again and again, until we finally get it. In this way:

We don't attract the soulmate we want, we attract the soulmate we need.

Our souls are so committed to our healing, transformation and flourishing, that they will keep bringing us the perfect people and experiences we need to propel us forward on our paths. If we keep looking for someone else to show up and alleviate us of our spiritual work, we may end up doing the opposite and attract partners and painful patterns until we master our soul-lessons. These lessons could include compassion, forgiveness, empowerment, self-love, self-worth, self-value, independence, resilience, and other higher values and lessons that honor the truth of who we are.

Soulmates and Past Lives

One of the main reasons we may confuse a soul-lesson mate for our ultimate soulmate is that both relationships can feel intensely euphoric at the beginning. One of the main reasons for this is that we may, in fact, have shared past lives with both partners, leading to the instant familiarity and feeling of having "known each other forever."

While we may share a long past-life history with either partner, there is a key distinction between the purpose of the two: soul-lesson mates typically reincarnate to heal and complete karmic patterns they incurred together, whereas ultimate soulmates come together after already evolving the relationship to a high level of spiritual love.

The good news is that we are not bound to repeat karmic cycles with soul-lesson mates if we commit to our own spiritual growth. If we do call in such soulmates, as long as we learn our lessons, we will be free to move forward.

We don't have to wait for our soul-lesson mates to learn their lessons either, as the Divine and their own spirits will lead them to more opportunities to learn their lessons in their own way and on their own time. We can bless and release them on their paths to their highest good, thanking them for the growth they brought us as we continue along our paths to become a match to our ultimate soulmates.

The Meaning and Purpose of Ultimate Soulmate Love

Even when we do the necessary inner work to unite with our divine, true soulmate—the one with whom we are meant to share the ultimate love—there will still be work and growth involved, it will just be at higher and ever-evolving levels.

It is essential to understand one thing:

Soulmate relationships are not perfect relationships—they are spiritual assignments.

Your soulmate is not a perfect person. Rather, they are the ideal partner to help you uncover your own divine perfection and your soul's highest capacity to love and be loved in return, and ultimately, to know divine love in human form.

Soulmates will give each other continuous opportunities to grow and surpass the limits of our love and compassion, so that we can learn to love as the Divine loves us—without conditions or expectations. Where our egos would choose guilt, blame, resentment, anger, frustration, and separation; our spirits will choose innocence, forgiveness, compassion, patience, and love.

In ultimate soulmate relationships, we will still trigger and challenge each other. The difference will be that we will be ready, willing and able to work through the challenges for our own and the relationship's evolution. And we will do so in kind, conscious, and compassionate ways, as a unit and with each others' best interests at heart. We will come together after earning essential soul-lessons, bearing the gifts of self-knowing, self-responsibility, and self-love; and by virtue of this, be focused on and committed to individual and mutual loving, honoring, growing and flourishing.

The Gift of Your Pre-Soulmate Time

Since you now know that there are many potential partners out there for you, and that the one you draw in will be the best one to contribute to your spiritual journey, the best thing you can do before your next relationship is to prepare for the most evolved spiritual partner: your ultimate soulmate. This soul being "the one" who comes into your life not to play out painful patterns, but to help you celebrate your growth and to contribute to it in the most loving, honoring, and conscious ways for both of your highest goods.

If you don't learn how to to heal your wounds, fill your voids, and meet your needs on your own, no one else will be able to do that for you. Even as a spiritual coach and healer, my role is to be a loving and supportive guide and facilitator, but the ultimate responsibility for transformation—and all the work required for it—rests with my client. Even the best therapist or most loving parent, friend, or partner cannot do for you what you are unwilling or unable to do for yourself.

Your soulmate is not going to fill what's missing, but mirror what already is.

They are not going to fulfill a need, but reflect back what you already have. Your job is to ensure that what you have in you is what you want reflected at you.

So let's start exploring what exactly is going on inside you, to ensure that what your soulmate mirrors and brings to you is your blissful, beautiful, and beloved self.

Step 3:

Uncover the Roots of Your Soulmate

Love Struggles

"It takes courage . . . to endure the sharp pains of self discovery rather than choose to take the dull pain of unconsciousness that would last the rest of our lives."
~ Marianne Williamson

One of the many contributions to the nature of human behavior and experience made by Dr. Sigmund Freud, the father of modern psychology, was his analogy of the iceberg to represent the conscious, pre-conscious and unconscious mind. According to Freud, the conscious mind, comprised of the endless things we are actively thinking, being aware of, and acting from (and trying to manifest with) is merely the tip of the iceberg. The preconscious mind is the level just below the surface, and houses the stored memories which we can retrieve with conscious intention.

However, the bulk of the iceberg represents the unconscious mind. This part is deemed the most inaccessible and the most significant in terms of explaining our external experiences. Therefore, the goal of Freudian psychotherapy—and the goal of our work in aligning with our desire for soulmate love—is to make the unconscious conscious so that we can break free of self-sabotaging patterns, and replace them with helpful ones that create what we actually want.

The concept—that most of what we experience on the outside is a reflection of what's going on inside—has since been widely expanded on in the personal and spiritual development fields, and is often referred to in the context of the law of attraction. According to research done by biologist Bruce Lipton, the unconscious mind is responsible for 95% of what we experience, while the conscious mind only represents 5%.

Our blocks to manifesting soulmate love—or anything we desire—have little to do with our outer conditions, and almost everything to do with our inner conditioning.

In my work helping clients uncover the root causes of their blocks to love and anything else they are consciously working to manifest, it is never surprising to find that their hidden beliefs and fears completely negate, contradict and conflict with their outer desires. Below are just some themes that have surfaced among my clients during this phase of the Manifest Soulmate Love Program:

Conscious Intention	Outer Block or Pattern	Uncovered Unconscious Block
I want to share my life with a wonderful companion.	Attracting unavailable or long distant partners.	"Being in a relationship will infringe on my freedom and independence. I will lose my autonomy in a committed relationship."
I want to find a partner who is ready and willing to get married.	Attracting only already married or committed men.	"All the great men are taken/married and the single ones won't want me."
I want a deep, soulful, life-long love.	Attracting partners but breaking up as soon as the relationship starts to develop and deepen.	"This is too good to be true. This can't be real. Love isn't safe. People can't be trusted. I don't want to get hurt."
I want a great partner that will bring me immense happiness and love.	Not attracting prospects, in spite of knowing many eligible singles.	"The kind of love I want isn't possible for me. I'm not worthy of it. It won't happen for me."
I want someone to love me unconditionally.	Attracting partners who take and take and take, and do not reciprocate.	"I am not enough. I have to earn their love, acceptance, and approval by proving myself to them and pleasing them."
I want a stable, committed, long-term relationship.	Dating online but not progressing to an in-person relationship.	"Love isn't safe, and I am afraid of being rejected and abandoned."
I want a best friend, passionate lover, and soulmate all in one.	Attracting passionless but deeply affectionate and emotionally fulfilling relationships, or ones with intense physical attraction but no deeper connection.	"It's not possible to have it all. Being with someone who loves me but I'm not attracted to is safe. Being with someone I'm attracted to is exhilarating but scary."

These are just some of the many patterns that I have uncovered in my work with clients, where we may go much deeper and make connections to previous relationships, childhood, and even past-life events that created these unconscious ideas in the first place.

No matter how hard we consciously hope and try to manifest love, if our unconscious (remember, 95% responsible) isn't supporting us, and worse, consists mainly of opposing fears and conflicting beliefs, what we end up getting is a reflection of our inner fears and blocks instead of what we outwardly desire.

Not just that, but as I mentioned, there could be karmic patterns at play that we are even more unaware of and may be very shocked to discover. And yet, we may quickly understand them as we make connections between past events and present patterns.

For example, you could have a deep-seated and unexplainable mistrust of people that is unrelated to experiences in this life. Through a past-life regression, you could discover that you were cheated on or betrayed by a parent, spouse, or other significant person. Left unhealed, the pain from that past life could be making you unconsciously weary of others in this one.

Another interesting pattern that shows up in past-life work—especially for those deeply committed to their spiritual paths—is uncovering that they were a monk or a nun in a past life, and took vows of celibacy that are still active, even though they are no longer relevant.

No matter how recent or far back our outer painful love experiences occurred, the important thing to remember is that healing doesn't happen in the past, it happens in the present. And what we do in the present is what creates our future.

If we want different results in the future, we need to change our past patterns in the present.

Our work is to uncover the damaging imprints that our negative experiences left on us and recognize how they are still creating struggle and discord for us today. From there, we can begin the process of healing, transforming, and reprogramming these patterns from their roots and ensuring that our unconscious beliefs are completely aligned with our conscious intentions.

In the case with my clients' common love-sabotaging beliefs that I shared in the previous chart, below are the new, positive affirmations we used to replace the false, fear-based ones. After answering the upcoming coaching questions to uncover your own negative beliefs around love, I highly encourage you to ask your heart and spirit to give you opposing and optimistic new beliefs with which to replace your old disempowering ones.

Old, Negative Unconscious Belief	New, Positive Belief and Affirmation
"Being in a relationship will infringe on my freedom and independence. I will lose my autonomy in a committed relationship."	"Being in a relationship with my soulmate will only add to my life, not take anything away. As two complete and independent people, we will honor and encourage each others' personal freedom and growth. I will have a beautifully balanced relationship in all ways."
"All the great men are taken/married and the single ones won't want me."	"There are endless amazing and available partners waiting for me. My divine right partner is searching for and ready for me. What is mine cannot be withheld from me. I am irresistibly desirable to those who are the best match for me. I can take my pick and I can choose my ultimate soulmate!"
"This is too good to be true. This can't be real. Love isn't safe. People can't be trusted. I don't want to get hurt."	"Love and happiness is my inherent truth. It is safe and right for me to love and be loved. I open to the trust and support of others. I am infinitely worthy of receiving love. I am worthy of being cherished and adored. I open to my spirit's capacity to feel safe and secure in all ways."
"The kind of love I want isn't possible for me. I'm not worthy of it. It won't happen for me."	"The kind of love I want is destined for me and I am divinely worthy of receiving it. It is Divine will that I be happy in all ways and I accept it. As a child of the Divine, I am equally worthy of all good and I graciously accept it. I am open for miracles and the best of all possibilities."

"I am not enough. I have to earn their love, acceptance, and approval by proving myself to them and pleasing them."	"Who I am is enough. Who I am is Divine. I am an expression of the Divine: infinitely loved, valued, and adored. I am inherently worthy because of who I am. I accept myself in all ways. I am worthy of and fully embrace my own self-acceptance, validation, and love. I only ever need my own approval, and I give this to myself in all ways. I love myself."
"Love isn't safe and I am afraid of being rejected and abandoned."	"I am safe, secure, and supported. I am whole and complete. I am infinitely worthy. I am endlessly loved. I am enough. I am divine. It is safe and right for me to love and be loved. Love is safe. I am safe."
"It's not possible to have it all. Being with someone who loves me but I'm not attracted to is safe. Being with someone I'm attracted to is exhilarating but scary."	"I am worthy of every good and complete happiness. The Divine's will for me is so much higher than mine and I open to it. I deserve to and will share the most profound mental, emotional, spiritual, and physical connection with my beloved soulmate. We are happy, connected, and blessed in all ways."

Ultimately, it's not as important or even necessary to delve into the past to find the origin of a sabotaging pattern. But it is essential that we be able to recognize the pattern and be willing to release it, so we can be free to move forward and create affirmative new patterns that support and honor us in all ways.

Let's help you start the process so you can prepare to release and reset all the patterns that are keeping you from manifesting the love and life you deserve.

Coaching Questions:

1. What do you believe are the reasons you are not yet with your soulmate? That is, what is the conscious "story" you have been telling yourself?
2. What painful experience or frustrating pattern have you incurred in past relationships?
3. What kind of inner beliefs could these patterns be reflecting back to you?
4. What messages about love, commitment, and men/women did you hear as a child, and perhaps still observe?
5. What examples of love and commitment did you and do you have? Are they positive and inspiring, or negative and discouraging?
6. What are you really afraid of?
7. What are you trying to protect yourself from?
8. What else?
9. Anything else?
10. Are you ready and willing to let these old stories, beliefs, and inner patterns go, or are they still protecting you and helping you feel safe?
11. Even if you are afraid, can you take a leap of faith and commit to healing them so you can move forward and manifest the love you deserve?

Beloved, I really hope your last answer was yes, because that is exactly what we will be helping you with next!

Step 4:

Heal and Transform Your Greatest

Barriers to Love

"Your task is not to seek for love, but merely to seek and find all the barriers within yourself that you have built against it."

~ Rumi

The mystic poet Rumi beautifully captured the heart of our true path back to love. But we need to go beyond just finding the barriers we have built up against it. Once found, we must heal, transform, and transcend these barriers in order to embrace and attract divine love.

After answering the questions in Step 3, you should now have some clarity around the inner beliefs that have contributed to the outer experiences which you want to heal. If you have not yet done so, please pause before reading any further and take as much time as you need to answer those questions before proceeding. Identifying the unconscious (and even conscious) patterns that are sabotaging your desire to manifest love is an essential preliminary step before breaking free and moving forward.

Once you have your answers, there is another important in-between step that needs to happen before you can release the pattern: to feel your feelings full-force.

Healing Through Feeling

In most law of attraction work, we are taught to be positive all the time, focus on what we want, and avoid any negativity, lest we block our desires. However, this idea is quite misguided because, as humans, we are going to experience blessings and challenges, and the natural emotional responses that come with them. Thus, such advice restricts us from doing the very necessary and healthy work of processing our raw, authentic emotions, no matter what they are. What's worse, instead of co-creating our dreams, repressing painful emotions ends up creating discord, disharmony, dissonance, and even disease, if we don't work through them.

Referring back to Step 3, you should now have some clarity about your inner fears and negative beliefs, and perhaps some insight as to where they stem from. In order to move beyond them, you first need to give yourself full permission to grieve all the pain they carry, because . . .

In order to heal your pain,

you must first feel your pain.

Powerful Practice: Write It Out to Let It Out

A safe, powerful, and healthy way to do this is by writing everything out uncensored. You can write to a person (please don't share it with them as this is just for you) or to yourself, your spirit, or the Divine. As long as you are somewhere private, feel free to swear, yell, cry, and scream as you express your deep, raw emotions—don't hold back! Once you have expressed everything out onto paper—all your rage, anger, sadness, grief, or any other repressed emotion buried within—you may already feel lighter as a result of allowing yourself to fully unleash your emotions. But we're not going to stop there . . .

Powerful Practice: Burn Your Old Story & Rise Anew From its Ashes

Now that you have released all your unconscious emotions on paper, the next step is to clear them from your energy and your life. One of my favorite rituals for this stage is to—*very carefully*—burn the damn paper.

Fire has always been known as the element of transformation and transmutation. Through fire, alchemists turn metal into gold—or, from a spiritual perspective—transform the darkness of ego into the light of truth.

This essential step of setting your story on fire will free reserves of energy and power you didn't even know you held. As you witness the deepest wounds of your past burn before you, your soul will rise like a phoenix from its ashes and be free for the next phase of your transformation.

Free Yourself With Forgiveness

After burning away your old story, the next most powerful step on your healing journey is the practice of forgiveness.

It can feel impossible to forgive when we are holding on to "rightful anger," because it gives us a sense of false power. However, in truth, we are not empowering ourselves at all if we still feel victimized by our wrongdoers, who did what they did because of the level of consciousness from which they were operating. Rest assured that through their actions, they created their own *karma* (the effect/consequence of past deeds, including the intention behind them) which their souls will ensure they face and balance in time. You do not need to concern yourself with them, but focus instead on freeing yourself and reclaiming your true power, dignity, respect, love, worth, and value.

If you still feel unready to forgive, remember this: You are not forgiving the person who hurt you, you are releasing the pain their actions continue to cause you, which are keeping you stuck as a victim instead of a free victor. And if you want to create the healthy and happy life that you deserve and the love you desire, you must be willing to forgive and release all that no longer serves you.

No matter how strong the venom of your past events, you have the right and responsibility to yourself to be free of their poisonous effects.

Only then will you be able to move forward with a clear mind, a healthy body, a happy heart, and a light spirit, and create the love and life you deserve.

Transcend Karma by Learning Your Soul-Lesson

Beyond truly forgiving, which is profoundly healing and transformative in itself, there is an additional step that can help you not just release your past pains, but transcend them. This is the commitment to learn the soul-lesson you were meant to learn.

Committing to learning the soul-lessons, especially from extremely painful experiences and patterns, will free you from that pattern not only for this lifetime, but for future ones as well, as you will no longer need to attract experiences to learn that lesson.

One of the greatest gifts of focusing your attention and intention on learning your soul-lesson is that instead of feeling victimized by the people involved, you feel grateful to them as your teachers, for they helped you progress and evolve on your spiritual growth journey (even if that was not their conscious plan).

If, by any chance, there is still a part of you that wants restitution—beyond knowing that we all must face the consequences of our actions on our soul journeys—rest in the knowing that your own freedom and happiness *are* the ultimate payback. Nothing is more rewarding than coming into your own power and joy, no matter what you have been through or what has been done to you.

While past-life healing work can help you learn your soul-lessons, it's not so much the process but your willingness and commitment to move forward that will create the shifts in your life. Even in my client work, sometimes we can release a pattern in a single session and sometimes, we need to keep peeling away more and more layers as the depths of the pattern become revealed through the healing work.

So please be patient with yourself, and know that you may need to repeat the process until you truly feel a shift within you, which will very quickly be evidenced by your new outer experiences.

Powerful Practice: Free Your Soul Ritual

Note: As you will need to close your eyes for the visualization, please read the instructions first. You may also wish to read all four parts of the ritual to best prepare for it.

Part 1: Release—Guided Visualization
When you feel ready to forgive and move forward with only the spiritual lessons, love, and growth, carve out some time for the following guided visualization:

Create a sacred space for yourself, perhaps playing healing music and lighting candles or incense. Sit in a comfortable posture, bring your awareness to your breath, and gently close your eyes. After a few moments of simply noticing your breath and getting centered, call on your guardian angels (we all have them) or any other spiritual guides with whom you connect.

Begin to imagine pure, luminescent white light fill your entire being and surround you in a bubble of sparkling light. Feel this bubble instantly and magically transport you into a sacred inner realm.

See yourself now sitting in a paradise-like ocean shore, breathing in the salty air, and feeling the warmth of the sun on your skin. As you sit here strong and centered, you are now greeted by all the souls that need your forgiveness.

They come before you one by one: Every single person who broke your heart or caused you pain, every role model of false and fear-based messages regarding love, every contributor to disempowering beliefs about yourself, others, love, and the universe. It is not their human self, but their own divine soul that sits before you, as willing to heal your shared past as you are.

At last, you are ready to be free, forgive, keep the soul-lesson, and move forward in all ways. You are unequivocally ready, willing, and able to do this with everyone and without exception.

As each soul sits before you, honor the divine light within them and thank them for their presence. Then ask them:

What lesson are/were you here to teach me?

Listen into your heart for the answer. Even if you don't feel you heard anything, keep breathing into your heart and trust that the answer has been given to and through your spirit.

Next, prepare to completely forgive and release them by saying:

I now completely forgive you in all directions of time.

I keep only the lessons and the love.

There is nothing unfinished between us.

You are free and I am free.

I bless and release you to your highest good.

After each soul shares the lesson they came to teach you, thank them, bless them, and release them. You can imagine placing them in a bubble of light and floating away when you are done.

Once you have forgiven everyone, walk into the healing waters of the magical ocean and let yourself bathe in it. Play and float in there until you feel purified and cleansed.

Step back out to the shore and feel yourself filled with and surrounded by light again. Come back into your bubble of light and fully back into your body.

Bring your awareness back to your breath. Bring both hands together in front of your heart, acknowledging and honoring yourself for having the courage to do this powerful, soul healing work. Thanking your spirit, the Divine and any angels or guides you connect with, open your eyes when you are ready.

Part 2: Transmute—Burning Ceremony

If you wish to go further or have a ceremonial final release, you can also write the below on a piece of paper and (very safely) burn it:

Even though I experienced pain with all these souls, in this sacred moment, I am willing to release it all and keep only the lessons and love. I ask that all karma between us be healed and forgiven through all of time. May there be nothing unfinished between us. They are free and I am free, and I bless and release them all to their highest good.

I now also release and surrender all that no longer serves me for my highest good. I now and forever reclaim and live from my own truth and power, and open to my spirit's highest capacity for self-love, respect, empowerment, worth, and value in all ways. I open to all the blessings I have always deserved and I know that it is safe and right for me to receive them. Amen/So be it.

Part 3: Cleanse—Healing Bath

It's a beautiful idea to even further seal in this ritual by following it with a healing bath: pour two cups of sea and/or Epsom salt and a few drops of essential oils if you have any (lavender, rose, and jasmine are lovely), and soak in these healing waters for fifteen to twenty minutes.

Part 4: Ground—Balancing Tips

Ground yourself after by balancing the intensity of the healing with something really light and fun, like a great meal with a friend, playing with a child or pet, or watching a comedy. Joyfully rest in knowing that you have just taken one of the most essential steps in healing your life and inviting your beloved.

Before you manifest your soulmate or any desire, be willing to face your past honestly, process it authentically, learn your lessons graciously, forgive everyone gracefully and move forward resiliently. As you step up to this level of spiritual strength and resilience, you will naturally clear the way for the next essential step on your path not just to soulmate love, but to every happiness: true self-love.

Step 5:

Master True Self-Love To Attract True Romantic Love

"You can search throughout the entire universe for someone who is more deserving of your love and affection than you are yourself, and that person is not to be found anywhere. You, yourself, as much as anybody in the entire universe, deserve your love and affection."

~Buddha

Now that you have faced your darkest feelings and deepest fears, forgiven everyone involved, reclaimed your power and reset your patterns—aligning your unconscious beliefs with your conscious desires—you are paving the path for a lifetime of self-love that will serve as the required foundation for anything you attract and everything you experience.

To ensure we operate from this foundation in all ways, it is essential to clarify a key area where most of us get stuck around self-love: Self-love is not just an idea to understand intellectually, it is a truth to know spiritually, practice mentally, embody emotionally and express physically.

You come from love, were made with love, are here to love and be loved, and will return to love.

Love is not something to seek from another, but the truth that you are trying to return to in your search for your soulmate. That's one of the main reasons that when we find our true soulmate, we feel like we are finally "at home" and can rest in this state of pure peace and bliss at last.

While forming this sacred connection with a fellow soul is a beautiful and worthy goal, what we are really longing to experience is to return home, and that home is our true inner state of perfect love and joy. While ultimate soulmate love will reflect back to us our own divine light, inherent goodness, and perfection; to attract such love, we must first return to our own inherent nature.

When I ask my clients what they would feel once they have their true soulmate, they all ultimately want the same things as the rest of us: to feel special, enough, safe, secure, supported, respected, accepted, understood, connected, adored, cherished, valued, honored, and, of course, loved. However, from a spiritual standpoint, we already are all these things and so much more! So our work with attracting the highest form of soulmate love is to first connect with the soulful love that is the truth of our own being.

Understanding Versus Embodying True Self-Love

As I explained earlier, self-love is not just a concept to comprehend, but a spiritual, mental, emotional, and physical way of embracing and expressing our true divine nature. It is about getting into the kind of relationship with ourselves that we are hoping to manifest with our soulmates. Before we can manifest love, we must first become our own beloved. To do this, we need to go way beyond conceptualizing self-love and get into tangible ways to experience it.

Ahead are the five levels of self-love in practice that will lead you to self-love mastery and soulmate love manifestation:

1: Self-love in Action Spiritually

On a spiritual level, our work is to reconnect with our divine nature and let it uplift and guide us along all the other levels of self-love.

One of the simplest and most powerful ways to return to our spiritual state of infinite love is to develop a deeper relationship with ourselves through a spiritual practice that most resonates with us, and to commit to this as if our lives depended on it.

One of the reasons my Manifest Soulmate Love Program is offered only to a small number of screened clients is because one of the main requirements is the willingness and ability to commit to a *sadhana* (a daily spiritual practice). I also give my clients two separate and very specific *mantras* (sacred chants) each to practice for forty days within our ninety-day journey.

As you commit to this journey of self-love and realization, I invite you to consider and create a sadhana of your own that works best for you. By connecting with your spirit and the Divine on a daily basis, you are inviting all the wisdom, truth, light, peace, blessings, and gifts of your own blissful nature to flow forth and unfold like a beautiful lotus flower, that pushes beyond the muddy waters around it and rises up, unfolding pure and untainted.

Here are some basic steps to start your own sadhana:

1. Decide on how much time you can start with (ten to thirty minutes a day is great).
2. Decide what your practice will consist of. I highly recommend meditation and prayer/calling in the

Divine in whatever way resonates with you. You can also include affirmations, gratitude, journaling, time in nature, or anything that helps you feel connected to your spirit.

3. Decide when and where you will sit for your practice. Try to ensure you have privacy and a clean, sacred space that honors your special time.
4. Commit to your sadhana every day no matter how brief, because daily practice is more important than duration.
5. Approach your practice with curiosity, commit to it diligently and enjoy it light-heartedly!

Once you establish a daily meditation or other spiritual practice, if you are open to it, you can experiment with adding one or more of these three practices to your sadhana:

1. Ask the question, *Who am I?* and meditate on it for ten minutes.
2. Chant the Kundalini mantra "Sat Nam" or repeat its translation "Truth is my identity" 108 times every day for forty days.
3. Chant the Sanskrit mantra "Ahem Prema" or recite its translation "I am Divine Love" 108 times a day for forty days.

Please note that since it takes forty days for the very specific, subtle, but powerful energetic, karmic, and spiritual effects to create a shift. If you skip one day, you will need to start over. As the ego gets very strong any time you are committing to spiritual transformation, it tends to do its best to sabotage you, especially towards the end of the forty days, so it is important to have a very disciplined and reliable way of committing to this. And if you need to start over, see it as part of the adventure and take a light-hearted, peaceful warrior approach to seeing it through!

2: Self-love in Action Mentally

In Steps 3 and 4, we discussed the essential role of our unconscious and conscious thoughts and beliefs in creating our outer experiences.

If you practiced the questions and exercises from those steps to help you uncover, clear, and realign your inner patterns so that they support the outer experiences you want, you are now much better equipped to observe and adjust your thoughts so that they reflect your truth, and not your ego.

That said, since most of our thoughts are "automatic," and studies have shown that we have on average between 50,000 to 70,000 thoughts per day, it would be impossible to monitor every single thought, especially as most of them happen in the background. However, what we *can* do is observe the themes of the more prominent and consistent thoughts we have.

This is another reason why I placed the self-love in action spiritually first, because developing a daily spiritual practice like mindfulness meditation eventually enables us to observe the patterns of our thoughts, so we can consciously respond instead of unconsciously react.

Developing this ability will not only help you build a loving and supportive relationship with yourself, but also help you become the conscious, kind, and compassionate partner that will be able to respond to the inevitable tests in any relationship— even ultimate soulmate ones—in the same way. And as mentioned in Step 2, our commitment to take responsibility for our own growth and respond to challenges in relationships with an aware and considerate approach evolves both us and our relationships.

With respect to self-love, our work here is to observe the dominant thoughts we have towards ourselves. Here are some questions to help with this:

Coaching Questions

1. How do you tend to talk to yourself throughout the day?
2. What is the tone of your inner dialogue?
3. How do you talk to yourself when something goes well?
4. How do you talk to yourself when something goes wrong?
5. How do you talk to yourself when someone says or does something unkind to you?
6. How can you turn your inner voice into a supportive ally and loving friend?
7. How you can speak to yourself the way you would to your soulmate?
8. How can you speak to yourself the way you would want your soulmate to speak to you?

Once you gain clarity on your general thought patterns and how you talk to yourself, commit to speaking to yourself the way you would to an innocent child, best friend, empowered goddess, or anyone you would only ever speak to with the utmost respect, love, and honor—because you are worthy of your own self respect, care, and love. So let every word you speak to yourself reflect that back to you, Beloved.

3: Self-love in Action Emotionally

As we commit to cultivating a spiritual connection with ourselves, where we learn to consciously observe our thoughts and respond with compassion, we will naturally come into a deeply nurturing, supportive, and loving relationship with ourselves.

One secret behind the law of attraction is that it doesn't just operate on the principle that our thoughts create our reality but, more accurately, that the consistent feelings and inner state that our repetitive, dominant thoughts create becomes our energetic essence, or vibration, and that it is ultimately our vibration that the universe responds to.

That is why when we are trying to manifest love but don't feel love for ourselves, we attract people who just reflect that back to us. And that is why it is key to feel unconditional, crazy, wild, wonderful, soulful love for ourselves, so that we vibrate and radiate this essence into the universe and draw in someone who will be a match to our elevated energy.

We want to uncover, identify, and replace any lack of feelings of self-love, worth, value, respect, and empowerment with their highest and fullest presence within our hearts and being.

Getting here takes more inner work, and here are some questions to help you assess and amplify your self-love vibration:

Coaching Questions

1. What would it feel like to love yourself?
2. What would it feel like when your soulmate loves you?
3. How can you start feeling this way now?
4. How can you start to feel this way more and more every day?

4: Self-love in Action Physically

Now that you are spiritually, mentally, and emotionally connecting with yourself in loving ways, it will become almost impossible to treat your body—the home of your divine spirit—any differently. In fact, as the sacred vessel for your eternal

44

spirit in this beautiful and blessed incarnation, your body is worthy of the deepest reverence and regard.

Although I provide a sacred feminine practice to help my clients unleash their irresistible and totally magnetic "inner Aphrodite" energy in this part of the program, you can awaken your inner divinity by fully honoring and enjoying your body in all ways.

This means everything from nourishing your body with delicious and nutritious food, fueling it with plenty of water and healthy fluids, respecting it by avoiding harmful substances, supporting it with daily, vigorous, joyful movement (the word "exercise" is so uninspiring!), beautifully dressing and adorning, resting it when tired, pampering it, playing with it, dancing with it, and very importantly, being extremely discerning of whom you share it with and how—only with someone who will respect, revere, and ravish it! As an expression and manifestation of the Divine, treat your body as such and nothing less, Beloved.

5: Self-love in Action in Your Life

No matter how much progress we make with cultivating self-love on a spiritual, mental, emotional and physical level, the true measure of just how much we love ourselves will always be revealed in our life choices.

One of the main ways to assess if we are being true when it comes to loving ourselves—or to realize that we perhaps aren't—is in how we allow ourselves to be treated by others.

With all the inner and practical work you followed in the prior steps, by now you might naturally be examining other parts of your life that are not in alignment with your true self-love, worth, respect, and value, and this is really wonderful!

It's very common at this point of the program for my clients to start getting "aha moments," followed by a lot of "Why have I been putting up with this?" questioning in various parts of their lives. The reason is that when we commit to honoring, loving, and respecting ourselves, we will—perhaps for the very first time—start noticing all other the parts of our lives where we haven't been doing so. More specifically, in the process of healing, transforming, and loving ourselves, we are stripping away all the parts of us that were not serving us, and therefore, become more authentic as our true, divine selves begin to emerge from within.

As such, we begin to notice other aspects of our lives that are not aligned with our values, priorities, passions, and soul's desires; and our divine and inherent right to their fulfillment.

If this examination is not yet happening for you, here are some questions to engage in this very necessary process so that you are ready to readjust your life to ensure every part of it aligns with your true Self:

Coaching Questions

1. How do I allow others to treat me?
2. Do I feel comfortable saying no when I want to?
3. Do I set healthy boundaries on my time and energy?
4. Do I allow myself to receive as much as I give?
5. Do I spend my time doing things aligned with my values, goals, and priorities, or do I support others people's instead?
6. Do I happily and regularly invest time, money, and energy on my passions and desires?
7. Do I know what I want and allow myself to go for it?
8. Do I expect the best for myself and settle for nothing less than what my divine self deserves?

Don't be afraid of the answers—be ignited and empowered by them. And know that you don't have to know *how* you will make any changes you need to, and you don't need to do anything drastic like suddenly quit your day job or cut off your family. Instead, stay committed to this self-inquiry and be willing to make healthy adjustments.

In your daily spiritual practice, keep asking your Higher Self to give you step-by-step guidance on how to make any necessary changes gently and gracefully, honoring everyone involved and ensuring everyone's highest good.

If you feel afraid to make any divinely guided changes because you fear the consequences, please remember that your safety, support, and supply come from your connection to the infinite Divine Source within you—not by anyone or any condition outside of you. Those are just the means through which you receive your support.

But if the things you need are not coming from means that honor you, you can ask your Spirit to empower you to make the necessary shifts through your inner guidance, and let the universe support you with signs and synchronicity at each step.

Since you already did intensive inner work through the first few steps, know how to take responsibility for your own happiness and practice self-love on all levels, you are now perfectly positioned to make empowered life changes and choices that will align with your new-found or amplified relationship with yourself and the universe. And you deserve to have a life that reflects back to your divine nature of pure love and divine worth in all ways.

Once you know this and commit to living in oneness with your own self-love, worth, value, and respect, you will know what you truly deserve in all ways, and ensure that you align your desires with nothing less. Which brings us to the next essential step to manifesting soulmate love.

Step 6:

Set Your Soul Standards to Invite Your

True Soulmate

"Your love should never be offered to the mouth of a stranger,
Only to someone who has the valor and daring
to cut pieces of their soul off with a knife,
Then weave them into a blanket to protect you."

~ Hafiz

Before discussing our next step, I have to take a moment to pause and acknowledge you, my Beloved. By making it this far, you have demonstrated a true commitment not only to manifesting your soulmate, but to your own healing, growth, and transformation. I realize the journey has been intense, but I hope you have felt lovingly supported in taking full responsibility for everything you want to change in your life. I really hope that you now feel like your own hero(ine), your own beloved, and your own soul partner.

If you feel you need to take some more time to create any other inner or outer shifts to ensure that you are centered in your own power, joy, and love, please know that it is more important to get there first than to keep progressing through the next steps. Because the next three steps are going to focus on calling in your soulmate, and we want to ensure that you are doing this from a strong foundation based on true self-love, respect, worth, value, excitement, and optimism, without any major fears or blocks in the way.

Of course, we will never be done with all our work because we are here to continually heal and grow, but it would be ideal for you to be reconnected to your true, divine Self before we start connecting with your true divine partner.

Once you know in your heart that even as you are taking steps towards deeper and greater self-love and joy each day, we can start to focus your energy and intentions on connecting with and inviting your beautiful soulmate.

As I shared earlier, the reason it was so essential to do the inner work of clarifying where you are, understanding the true nature and purpose of soulmate love, identifying and releasing your inner barriers, and then mastering true self-love, is because we want to ensure you align with the highest level of soulmate love after all this hard work.

If you feel excited and empowered to send out your invitation to your beloved, you are now ready for the next secret to inviting in your best possible soulmate:

In order to receive the highest level partner, you need to give your highest level standards.

You have always deserved the most loving partner, but now that you have done deep inner healing and self-love work, you are much better aligned with this partner. Still, you want to check if there is any part of you that doesn't feel worthy of the most kind, loving, and wonderful partner, and then retrace the steps and readjust inside and out until you do.

From your newly formed attitude that you deserve the best and are ready to receive it, your next step is deciding what exactly that looks like for you. We all have our own preferences when it comes to what we seek in a partner and relationship, and based on our past experiences, we may (and should!) be very clear on what we want and don't want. For example, if your last partner was unfaithful, you will, of course, want to attract someone who is loyal, honest, and committed.

Powerful Practice: Connect With The Essence of What You Seek

Use your contrasting experiences of the past (the things that didn't serve you) to come up with what you want instead. Wherever you were not honored in past relationships, now you can put a firm foot down and command the highest standards for yourself to manifest the soulmate with whom you can share the highest level of love and bliss. Then, go further by elevating these standards with even greater *soul standards*. What do I mean by soul standards?

When you connect with the spiritual essence of the outer quality you are seeking from your partner, you are connecting with your soul's standards rather than your ego or more human standards. For example, if you want someone who is very successful because your last partner was financially dependent on you, what your soul wants from this is likely a sense of freedom, support, respect, and security, which you can start feeling now instead of waiting for someone to make you feel.

The magic is that once you feel the essence of your soul standards within yourself, you become the perfect vibrational match for not just a partner, but for other blessed circumstances that will reflect that back to you!

Your job is to get crystal clear on what you want, know that you deserve it, and then let the universe know you are ready for your divine love by feeling the feelings *now*.

Powerful Practice: Activate Your "Love Corner"

Once you have clarity on your soul standards—the ultimate, deep, positive and affirming feelings and states you want to experience with your beloved—go ahead and tell the universe very clearly that this is what you are ready for and that nothing less will do.

A fun and effective exercise for this is writing your soul standards on a paper and creating a special "love corner" in your bedroom where you can place it.

Create this area in the furthest right corner of your bedroom from your door. That is, when you stand at your bedroom door, whatever corner is furthest back and to the right—according to feng shui (the art of harnessing positive chi/energy in your environment)—is your love corner. You can also do this in the furthest right corner of your home's main door, which is your main love corner. It's a great idea to add things in pairs to represent "couple" energy in these corners.

When I was ready for love and used the law of attraction tools the right way (there is absolutely a wrong way to use them) I placed two rose quartz crystals, two synthetic red roses, two pink candles, and a beautiful large statue of Cupid & Psyche in a sacred embrace in my love corner, along with timeless love poetry books.

I remember my younger sisters making fun of my "new age" practices. But, when they saw that just three months later I had manifested Eric—my amazing soulmate and husband—guess who started coming by and asking about crystals and love corners? Let's just say now they are a lot more open-minded now!

Powerful Practice: A Prayer/Call to Invite Your True Soulmate

Whether or not you decide to create a dedicated love corner, here is a prayer or call you can use once you have your "soul standards for my soulmate list" ready:

Dear Divine/Universe/God (use whatever word resonates most with you),

I now ask for your fullest support in bringing me the most beautiful, wonderful, and evolved soulmate, one with whom I can share the greatest love and continue my greatest growth, as we both support and honor each other. I ask that you help me release any remaining patterns that could keep me from calling in my truest soulmate, and that you help me gently and joyfully align with my beloved. I am willing to learn any remaining lessons I need to in preparation for our divine union.

I ask that you elevate even my soul's standards, and help me align them with Your greatest and highest standards for me, for what You know I deserve. Thank you for letting me be completely prepared mentally, emotionally, spiritually, physically and in every part of my life to receive this great love and be a divine match to my most wonderful partner. Thank you for bringing us together so that we may know Your love for us and through us. May we be blessed as we become the greatest blessing for each other, healing, growing, and flourishing in all ways for all our days. Amen/So be it.

Stating your intentions to the Divine as you connect with your own divine essence will send out a beautiful, clear, and powerful message to the entire universe that you are ready for the highest spiritual partner, and that you are not settling for anything less. You are committed to learning any remaining lessons you need to, and have also asked the Divine to help you do so gently and swiftly as you prepare for such a love. As long as you stay true to your Self and trust in the Divine, you have opened to miraculous ways for the universe to deliver!

Step 7:

Partner With The Divine To Receive

Your Soulmate

"By giving you receive. But to receive is to accept, not to get.
It is impossible not to have, but it is possible not to know you have."
~ From "A Course in Miracles"

Beloved, after all your courageous work in clearing your inner barriers, reclaiming and living with true self-love, and stating your soul standards to the universe, your work will still continue, but now, the focus will be on joyfully partnering with the Divine to manifest your soulmate in magical and miraculous ways!

As I have discussed throughout, our soulmates and everything we attract reflect our inner state or vibration back to us. If we are coming from a place of wanting, needing, and longing for love and companionship, we will get more wanting, needing, and longing. We now know that instead of this clingy energy—which will repel the wonderful soulmate we desire and attract more soul-lesson mates instead—it is in our best interest to manifest our beloveds from a place of inviting, sharing, and enriching.

Since you have journeyed through all the previous steps, you are now in the best position to build on the foundation of soulful love and empowered standards by elevating your vibration to an even higher level, one that will help you attract your ultimate soulmate and many other unimagined blessings.

A Powerful Energetic Shift to Attract Love

Even though we may be filled with self-love and ready for soulmate love, there is a very powerful additional energetic shift we can make to propel us forward on our path to uniting with our beloved:

One of the most powerful energetic shifts we can make to receive soulmate love, is to freely give soulful love.

Since you can't get what you don't already have within you, and since you only get what you radiate, the single most powerful shift you can make after stepping into your self-love and worth is to fall in love with your life, and become a channel of love in the world.

Love is your truest, purest essence. When you feel, share, and practice love in any and every way you can, you are actually living most fully and truly from your deepest Self, and there is no greater joy than that.

This means putting love into every intention and action, which imbues and uplifts every outcome with your love. Of course, this does not mean forcing yourself to feel loving when you have any negative emotions show up—as discussed in Steps 3 and 4, it is essential to always honor, feel, and process our feelings. It means that as we stay true to ourselves, we will let love be our highest priority. This will actually help us with difficult people and circumstances as well, because after processing our feelings, we can always ask *What would love do?* to gain guidance on how to respond. And as we learned in Step 4 about self-love, sometimes love will make necessary healthy changes while respecting everyone involved.

Unconditionally loving others never means we unconditionally accept their unloving actions, and it is our divine right and responsibility to love ourselves and lovingly assert our values, needs, and standards as we live with fully awakened hearts.

The Magic of Giving

At this point, I always find that as my clients start living with a free flowing love, open hearts, and high soul standards, they start to experience not only an inner fulfillment, joy, and bliss that they never felt before, but they start experiencing miracle after miracle in every part of their lives. Relationships heal. People will stop them on the street to say or do something kind (like give them flowers!). Strangers will write poems for them. Dream jobs fall into their laps. Money shows up from the most unexpected places. They form new amazing friendships. People start going out of their way to offer support, love, and opportunities. All this is simply a natural reflection of the love that they are so freely experiencing and expressing.

Whatever we put out comes back to us, and love has a way of coming back manifold.

When we unleash the infinite source of love within us, the Source of all love showers us with infinite blessings.

We begin to glow as our true light shines through us, and this energy makes us irresistible to miracles and manifestations, including our beloved soulmates.

Not just that, but by emanating love and sharing it into the world, we become energetically aligned with the highest spiritual partner, one who will also be as loving, fulfilled, and complete on their own. As we come together as two whole, complete, fulfilled beings, centered in and radiating infinite love before we even meet, the love we share as a couple is simply divine. We come to share the highest manifestation of spiritual love, where instead of trying to get our ego needs met and unconscious wounds healed, we see and celebrate the divine within each other, keep each others' best interests at heart, and commit to elevating each others' happiness and individual journeys.

My husband Eric and I are often asked how our love and relationship become stronger and deeper with time. The simple secret to our happiness as a couple is that we take responsibility for our happiness as individuals. Because of this, we see each other as a blessing every day, never taking for granted that even though we are married, we choose every day to share our lives and ourselves with each other, and what a privilege, honor, and blessing that truly is.

We are committed to growing, learning, and flourishing together. Since we don't expect from the other anything that we cannot first give to ourselves, we ensure that we are centered in our divine joy and love, and from this place of fullness and fulfillment, we have nothing to take but only to offer. And in our offering to each other, we receive with such gratitude, and aim to keep out-giving and out-loving each other, continuously flowing onwards and upwards, instead of spiraling backwards and downward as we often do in soul-lesson relationships.

When we do the inner work and get to a place where we are channeling love into the universe, the universe returns this love back to us a thousand times over. Our job is to know and love ourselves as Divine beings, share our love and light in the world, and then magically unite with our beloved in divine and perfect timing, allowing the universe to do its part in bringing us together. If there is anything beyond our inner work that we need to do, we will be guided to take inspired action to meet our soulmates.

In the meantime, we can go on living our lives with the greatest joy, sharing the soulful love we already have within, as we welcome soulmate love along the way.

Powerful Practice: Loving Kindness Meditation

A beautiful way to become a channel of love is by practicing the loving kindness or "meta" meditation from the Buddhist tradition, which helps cultivate unconditional love and compassion for ourselves and all beings.

You can add this to your existing daily meditation practice. I love to start my day sending out love and light to all beings, so I always end my regular morning meditation with the meta meditation and chant some closing mantras to seal my practice.*

*I offer a free "Infinite Love" meditation MP3 download where I guide you through the entire meta meditation process on my website at http://www.FlourishingGoddess.com/infinite-love-meditation-mp3-download.

Here are the steps for this beautiful practice:

Step 1: Sit in meditation and rest your awareness on your heart. After connecting with your breath, begin to feel love for yourself radiating from your heart to your entire being. If you are more visual, you can imagine pink or golden light radiating through you from your heart.

Silently affirm, May I be free from suffering and filled with love and peace.

Step 2: Now think of someone you love—a family member, friend, pet, anyone dear to you. Picture them in front of you and send them love in whatever way feels best to you. Keep calling in all your loved ones, or see them as a group in front of you and send them all love and kindness. Silently bless them by saying, May you be free from suffering and filled with love and peace.

Step 3: Now think of people you are not so close to, like acquaintances, and send them the same love and kindness, ending with the blessing, May you be free from suffering and filled with love and peace.

Step 4: Now send love and kindness to those with whom you may still have difficulty, without exception. Remember, you are not condoning their behavior but, for just this moment, acknowledging and connecting with their divine essence and your oneness with their soul, since we are all one in truth. It's okay if you have resistance. Just do your best and be kind and forgiving with yourself. No matter what, silently bless them by saying, May you be free from suffering and filled with love and peace.

Step 5: Keep extending your love out to everyone in your country and the entire world, and then to all beings everywhere. You can imagine pink light beaming from your heart and shining through the entire universe. Silently affirm, May all beings everywhere be free from suffering and filled with love and peace.

Step 6: Feel love from the entire universe radiate and flow back to you. Feel it center and rest in your heart. Begin to connect with your heartbeat and breathe again. Feel your feet, wiggle your toes, bring your hands together in front of your heart and when you are ready, open your eyes with a smile on your face.

This meditation will fill your life with more love, healing, and miracles than you can know, blessing you as you become a blessing in the world. And of course, help you become a magnet of love as you channel infinite love!

Here are some questions to further help you put love into action:

Coaching Questions

1. How do you express your love to the people in your life?
2. How can you practice even greater love in action?
3. How can you serve, share, and care, bringing blessings to yourself and others?
4. What small thing can you do each day to express love?

As you become a clear and pure channel divine of love, the universe will automatically start reflecting this back to you in countless and magical ways. And since you have given it your intention and invitation for soulmate love, it will bring you the love you are emanating in miraculous ways, on the wings of angels . . . as long as you trust it to, which is the next and final step in manifesting soulmate love and anything we desire.

Step 8:

"Let Go & Let God" To Let Love In

*"We can only learn to know ourselves and do what we can, namely,
Surrender our will and fulfill (Spirit's) will in us."*
~St. Teresa of Avila

After all this work of healing our barriers against love, mastering self-love, inviting the highest soulmate love, and radiating divine love, the only block to receiving love from this point forward will be our attachment to it.

How do we know we are ready for love?
When we no longer need it.

A Course in Miracles says, "Infinite patience produces immediate results." This means that when we completely release our attachment to when or how our desires will come into form, and we know without question that what is ours cannot be withheld from us. We have nothing at all to worry about or wait for. We have total faith. With such faith in our good, and in the loving Creator who wills nothing but our highest good, we can trust in the wisdom that created us to manage all the details of turning our dreams into reality.

To get to this state of grace means we have mastered the art of true and total surrender. Surrender does not mean that we don't do anything or that we become complacent. It means that any action we take comes from a place of inner guidance, joy, and inspiration. Co-creation is, after all, a divine partnership between us and Spirit.

In surrendering, we are committing to do our part by aligning our intentions and actions with the Divine's highest will for our greatest good, and then hand over the outcomes that we may receive our highest good, in profound ways, and in perfect timing.

Surrender means we are living in faith,

and know that as we believe, so shall we see.

Powerful Practice: Balancing Intention, Action & Surrender

To practice the art of surrender on a practical level, we must harness the divine feminine and masculine principles of trusting and acting, listening and responding, being and doing. This means that as you are living your life to the fullest, and taking full responsibility for your self-love and happiness, you are paying attention to your inner guidance and outer signs to meet your beloved. You may be guided to go to a certain place or to try something new, but if you feel a positive, peaceful, and persistent inner nudge to go for it, go for it.

Your intuition is God's way of helping you help Him to help you.

I remember the first night I properly met Eric was on a New Year's Eve. A friend had invited me to her party, but I was too down and depressed to go. I sat home indulging in my misery, until I very clearly heard an inner voice almost shout, *Enough of this! Get up, get ready, and go.* The voice was so clear and firm, and suddenly, it felt like a powerful and benevolent force almost took over and gave me the strength to get my sulky self to the party.

It was that night that I connected with Eric for the first time. Though it would be months before we would come together, given the journey I was on, following my guidance throughout the year to get out of the house and be around friends allowed me to get to know how organically wonderful Eric was. By the time I had fallen in love with myself and became ready for soulmate love, our union happened instantly.

Our intuition, which is a sacred feminine gift, guides us to take inspired action, a sacred masculine gift.

As we listen to and follow the guidance from Spirit within, we work in consort with it to create our desires without.

This is another reason why developing and maintaining a daily spiritual practice, taking loving care of ourselves, and becoming pure vessels of love is so essential in attracting our divine soulmates: it helps us hear, trust, and follow our intuition, which helps us work with the benevolent forces of the universe to unite with our beloved.

63

Even as we do, there may be times that we step into resistance and out of surrender. Any time we start to feel doubtful in any way, we have chosen fear over faith. While it's perfectly human for this to happen, the way back is always through our spirits. All we need to do when fear steps in is take a stand against it with love. We can pause, take a deep breath, meditate, pray, and ask the Divine to help bolster our faith when we slip into doubt. We can ask for our perception to be lifted so that we may see the situation from our spirit's wisdom rather than our ego's lies.

As we stay centered in our own truth, self-love, soul standards, and total surrender, we place ourselves in the most ideal and inviting space to let every good from the Divine and every form of love to fill and bless our lives. Love is who we are and what we are here for.

And as you move forward from here and wonder what's next, know this:

It is not *your* desire to experience soulmate love as much as it is *Spirit's* desire that you know *Its* love for you. It is the Divine's will that you know nothing else, because from a spiritual standpoint, nothing else is real anyway.

So if you ever think from now onward that it is a little old for you to be wishing for love upon a star, know that it is, in fact, your own soul desiring to experience its fullest and truest essence and expression through true love.

Your ultimate soulmate is just one way in which you are meant to experience this love, but the ultimate "one" to share this with is already within you—is *you*.

Conclusion:

Ready for Love

On a journey that began to find your soulmate, it is my deepest prayer that you ended up finding and falling in love with your Self.

That you discovered where you really were in your readiness for soulmate love.

That you learned what soulmate love is (a spiritual relationship) and isn't (a perfect relationship).

That you had the courage to face and heal your greatest barriers to the deepest love.

That you took back your power and reclaimed your inherent nature of divine self-love.

That you uplifted the desires you have for your partner to your soul's standards and the Divine's highest will for what you deserve.

That you committed to becoming a pure, radiant channel of love in the world, focused on giving rather than getting.

And at last, that you have learned that your only work now is to be in blissful surrender as you continue to live in oneness with your spirit, and let Spirit guide you on the path to your divine right partner, your ultimate soulmate.

You have come to know your own soul, so you are ready to know your soulmate.

You have become your own beloved, so you are ready for your beloved.

You have done the inner preparation to welcome the outer manifestation.

It is my absolute faith that you will be united with your blessed soulmate, so that you both may live your lives on Earth as it is the Divine's will for you in heaven: with complete bliss and total love. So be it. Amen.

Manifest Soulmate Love Affirmations

My Beloved, now that you have journeyed through the eight essential steps to attract your ultimate soulmate and experienced your own transformation along the way, I am delighted to share with you the following divinely channeled affirmations to further support you on your path.

Because it can be so much easier and more effective to hear the affirmations—and as a thank you for inviting me to guide you on your soulmate love journey—I am even more excited to share that I have created a free MP3 where I recite the below affirmations so that you can listen to them whenever you wish.

To receive these Guided Affirmations MP3 please click this link: visit:

http://FlourishingGoddess.com/msl-ebook-love-
affirmationsbonus

A powerful way to work with affirmations is to say each one three times: First out loud, next a little quieter, and finally, silently.

Breathe into your heart between each one, and *feel the essence* of the words as you repeat them:

I am ready for love.
I am ready for the highest manifestation of ultimate soulmate love.
I release all barriers that could block me from soulmate love.
I forgive everyone who ever hurt me.
I forgive my mother and bless her on her path.
I forgive my father and bless him on his path.
I forgive all past romantic partners and bless them on their paths.
I forgive all friends and bless them on their paths.
I forgive everyone, without exception, that I may be free in all ways.
There is nothing unfinished or unbalanced between us anymore.
I am free. They are free.
I am free to welcome love.
I am free to heal myself and I do.
I am free to love myself and I do.
I am free to respect myself and I do.
I am free to honor myself and I do.
I am free to value myself and I do.
I am free to empower myself and I do.
I am free to adore myself and I do.
I am free to cherish myself and I do.
I am free to support myself and I do.
I open to my spirit's highest perception of who I am.
I am a child of the Divine.
I am infinitely loved.
I come from love.
I am here to love.
I stand in and live from my divine truth, worth, and love.
I love myself in all ways.
I love myself unconditionally.
I love and honor my body.
My body is a temple of my soul.

My body is sacred and beautiful.

My body deserves to be respected and ravished.

I nourish, appreciate, and enjoy my body every day in every way.

I treat myself as I would have my beloved treat me.

I am my own beloved.

All the love I seek is already within me, and I share it effortlessly and joyfully.

I am a channel of divine love.

I am divine love.

I welcome divine soulmate love.

I welcome the highest and most evolved spiritual partner.

I am ready to share, grow, and flourish together.

I welcome the Divine's total support in bringing my soulmate and I together.

I surrender to perfect timing.

I have infinite patience and trust in divine timing.

I am open to miracles and magic.

I live in surrender and bliss.

I stay true to my higher self and follow my inner guidance.

I believe soulmate love is possible for me and surrender any resistance.

I open to my spirit's capacity to know that soulmate love is destined for me.

I open to my spirit's capacity to prepare me for ultimate soulmate love.

I open to my spirit's capacity to elevate me to the greatest love.

I trust in the Divine to guide us to each other.

I know this love is coming.

My soulmate and I are already connected in spirit, and I open to uniting on Earth.

I open to the Divine's highest will to be fulfilled for my love and life.

My will is one with God's, whose will for me is infinite peace,
    bliss, and love.
My soulmate and I are blessed.
My soulmate and I are blissful.
My soulmate and I are one with Spirit.
My soulmate and I are one.
So be it. So it is.

About the Author

Syma Kharal is an international sacred feminine and spiritual coach, healer, speaker, yoga teacher and #1 Amazon bestselling author. She is dedicated to empowering soulful women heal their deepest wounds, manifest their boldest dreams and flourish in every way.

Syma immersed herself in the healing arts at the age of 14 to overcome the deeply damaging effects of extensive abuse and trauma. In addition to healing herself, her intensive spiritual work led her to co-create a life she never dreamt possible: leaving a toxic corporate career to follow her calling, manifesting and marrying her soulmate, transforming women's lives through her heart's work, and traveling the world with her beloved husband.

She loves nothing more than supporting fellow sisters to do the same—to transcend disempowering patterns, reclaim their full feminine power, and step fully into the Goddesses they truly are.

Receive Syma's free, "Awaken Your Inner Goddesses" guided meditation MP3 at:
FlouishingGoddess.com

Connect with her on:
Facebook: facebook.com/FlourishingGoddess
Instagram: instagram.com/FlourishingGoddess
YouTube: youtube.com/FlourishingGoddessTV

Made in the USA
Middletown, DE
28 April 2022

64885046R00046